AF143857

BOOK ANALYSIS

By Maria Aalto

NW

BY ZADIE SMITH

Bright
≡Summaries.com

ZADIE SMITH

ENGLISH WRITER

- **Born in London in 1975.**
- **Notable works:**
  - *White Teeth* (2000), novel
  - *On Beauty* (2005), novel
  - *Swing Time* (2016), novel

Zadie Smith is an English writer of fiction and non-fiction. Her first novel, *White Teeth*, was highly successful and established her as one of the most prominent writers of her generation. Her successive works have helped to consolidate this.

Smith is the daughter of a Jamaican mother and an English father. She grew up in London, which is the setting for many of her works of fiction, and studied English literature at the University of Cambridge. She is an acclaimed writer who has received several prizes for her books, including the Whitbread First Novel Award for *White Teeth* in 2000 and the Orange Prize for Fiction for *On*

Beauty in 2006. Smith's literary style varies from different forms of realism to highly experimental fiction. She is known for her social satire, sharp observations and lively dialogues, and for her handling of subjects such as race, class, immigration, gender, identity and religion.

NW

PORTRAITS OF LIFE IN NORTHWEST LONDON

- **Genre:** novel
- **Reference edition:** Smith, Z. (2013) *NW*. London: Penguin Books.
- **1ˢᵗ edition:** 2012
- **Themes:** social class, gender, sexuality, identity, multiculturality, race, adulthood, time

NW portrays life in northwest London. The novel's title designates a postcode of this area, which is the centre of its characters' world. The characters, now adults, have grown up in a council estate in the area, and the novel follows the turns their lives have taken and shows how their background keeps defining them in many ways. Leah Hanwell, Natalie Blake and Nathan Bogle were in school together, but their current lives are very different from one another. However, their common past and social background remains significant.

Smith explores themes such as social class, immigration, multiculturality, gender, adulthood and the passage of time in this novel. *NW* is stylistically remarkable, and the multitude of different kinds of people in London is matched with a variety of literary devices. Smith experiments with mixing different narrative techniques: relatively traditional third-person narration, stream of consciousness and stage direction-like passages find their places in the novel, along with unusual punctuation and use of space on the pages of the book, creating a whole which is fragmented but interconnected.

SUMMARY

VISITATION

The novel is divided into sections which focus on different characters. The first section, Visitation, depicts the life of Leah Hanwell, a Londoner of Irish descent. At the beginning of the novel, Leah is alone at home. She opens the door when a distressed-looking woman, Shar, comes asking for help. Shar claims her mother has been taken to hospital because she had had a heart attack and she needs help. Shar and Leah realise they know each other (although not well) from school. Leah lends Shar some money, and Shar promises to pay her back the next day. Leah's husband, Michel, and her mother Pauline think that Leah was being naïve when she gave Shar the money. Leah is aware of the possibility that Shar might be lying, but prefers to act with empathy towards her. It turns out that Michel and Pauline were right: Shar is a drug addict, and was lying about the nature of her distress and does not pay Leah what she owes. Leah feels betrayed, but also wants to help Shar. She works at a local organisation that distributes money to charities and small non-profit organisations, and suggests she could help Shar find help for her problem, but Shar does not want this kind of help.

Leah has grown up on the same council estate where she now lives. Compared to Shar she seems to be successful in her life, as she has a degree, a job and a loving husband. However, when compared to her childhood best friend Natalie Blake (who used to be called Keisha), who works as a barrister and has married up, Leah has stayed closer to her working-class origins. Leah and Natalie have remained friends, and Leah and Michel often visit Natalie and her husband, Frank, but Leah feels that their lives and social circles have become too different. Besides the differences in their social status, Leah and Natalie are separated by motherhood: Natalie has two children, and Leah does not have any. In fact, Leah does not want any, although she does not tell this to her husband. At the beginning of the novel Leah is pregnant, but she keeps this a secret and finally has an abortion. After this she secretly takes a contraceptive pill. Michel would like to have children and move on with their lives. Leah does not want to move on, as she equates it with ageing and ultimately with death. However, she does not share these thoughts with other people, and attempts to behave as is expected of her.

GUEST

This section focuses on Felix Cooper's experiences. Felix too lives in northwest London, but does not know Leah and Natalie. He is a black, working-class man. He has had a difficult life and has struggled with drug addiction, but he seems to be getting his life on track. He has stopped taking drugs for a while now and is in love with Grace, a woman who encourages him to make positive changes in his life. In the course of the day that is described in the novel, Felix visits his father, buys an old car he plans to repair and goes to break up with an old lover from his drug-fueled past (whom he has not seen for a while). On his way back he tries to ask two men sitting on the tube to move so that a pregnant lady can sit down, but the men respond negatively, and Felix gives her his seat. When Felix is almost home, he is mugged and killed, apparently by the same men he asked to move earlier.

HOST

This section is dedicated to Natalie Blake's experiences. Natalie, who was originally called Keisha, comes from a working-class family of Caribbean origin. Natalie/Keisha and Leah have been friends since early childhood. This section shows how the two of them grew up together, and what makes them close, even though in the present of the novel they are going through a period in which they seem less connected than before. Keisha was always a smart and ambitious child, determined to succeed and to finish any project that she starts. In her youth she is torn between her religious family background and her curiosity about other ways to live and her awakening sexuality. When Keisha finishes school, she goes to study law with her boyfriend Rodney Banks. Rodney is hardworking, religious and kind to Keisha, but also somewhat boring. Keisha eventually becomes less conservative and her relationship with Rodney comes to an end. She enjoys her freedom and has some more adventurous relationships before finally settling down with Frank De Angelis, who is of Italian and Caribbean origin and much wealthier than

Keisha. It is during the period of becoming a successful law student that she changes her name as part of a process of reinventing herself. After her studies and after a brief period of having a small paralegal job, Natalie becomes a successful barrister. She is now married to Frank, and the two of them buy a nice house and finally have two children. It seems like Natalie has achieved everything she had worked so hard for, but she is secretly restless. She seeks couples to have sexual relations with online, and goes by her old name for these encounters (many of which do not lead to actual sexual relations). Frank discovers her infidelity and confronts her. After an argument Natalie leaves her house, taking nothing with her.

CROSSING

This section follows Natalie as she walks in northwest London after her argument and meets an old classmate, Nathan Bogle. Nathan has become a drug addict who lives on the street. He and Natalie/Keisha, who started their life in the same school, have gone on to have very different lives, but they spend some time together and smoke cannabis together. Natalie remembers that her friend Leah was in love with Nathan when they were children. After spending some time together on what seemed like amicable terms, Nathan tells Natalie that she cannot understand what life is like for him, and has no place talking to him and judging him. They keep talking, but now on less good terms. Natalie contemplates jumping off a bridge but does not.

VISITATION

The last part of the novel returns to the first story line, Visitation. Natalie's relationship with Frank seems to be coming to an end, as they take turns to be with their children. Michel has found out that Leah has been taking contraceptive pills behind his back, and Leah seems to be having some sort of breakdown. She lies in the sun, although she usually avoids sun because her skin burns easily, and does not respond when Michel talks to her. Michel has called Natalie asking her to come over. Natalie tells Michel that Leah loves him but does not want children. It is not clear where Leah and Michel's marriage is headed, but Natalie gets Leah talking again. The conversation turns to the killing of a man in the area (the victim is Felix). Natalie thinks Nathan Bogle is involved. The novel ends with Natalie and Leah calling the police to tell them about Natalie's suspicions.

CHARACTER STUDY

Leah is one of the novel's main characters. She is a red-haired woman of Irish origin. She grew up on a council estate in northwest London, and still lives in the area as an adult. In terms of social mobility, she has climbed up slightly. She has a degree and lives in a flat that is "nice for council" (p. 8). The fact that she is living in a council flat not far from where she grew up and works for a local organisation means that essentially, nothing much has changed (especially as her childhood family already was slightly better off than many other families in her area). When compared to her former classmates from university, who are now bankers and lawyers, Leah has not been successful: "Meanwhile Leah, a state-school wild card, with no Latin, no Greek, no maths, no foreign language, did badly – by the standards of the day – and now sits on a replacement chair borrowed six years ago from the break room, just flooded with empathy" (p. 32). Leah, however, values other things above material success: love, friendship and empathy, for example. Leah, unlike her husband and her friend Natalie, is not very concerned about moving forward with her life. In fact, she fears change, adulthood, aging and having children. This has to do with her fear of death. Leah struggles with many difficult feelings: she fails to live up to the expectations of her society and those close to her. Moreover, she does not want to live up these expectations. She is now in her mid-30s, but would like to live as if she would be young forever. She is aware of the irrationality of this, and does not voice these feeling to others. On top of her personal struggles, she is flooded with feelings of empathy towards people in her part of London who are less fortunate than her.

NATALIE/KEISHA BLAKE

Natalie Blake is Leah's childhood friend. She comes from a religious working-class family of Caribbean origin. Despite being a black woman from a working-class home, Natalie is very successful in her life. She is intelligent, hardworking, goal-oriented and organised. She studies law and has a successful career. She reinvents herself to suit her middle-class aspirations, she even changes her name from Keisha to Natalie. She also marries a man who is from a rather wealthy family, buys a house and has two children with him. Her friend Leah describes her current circumstances by saying: "Lives just over there, in the posh bit, on the park. She's a lawyer now. Barrister. What's the difference?" (p. 10). Although everything seems perfect, Natalie is not content with her life. She seeks sexual encounters with people she meets online, although many of these meetings do not actually end in sex. When Frank, Natalie's husband, catches her cheating, her seemingly ideal existence comes to an end of a kind. Interestingly, Natalie uses her old name and dresses like someone from her original background might do during her secret encounters. This suggests that she is not ready give up on her old self and background. It is, however, not a simple question of reviving a past self, as Natalie was religious and did not have many sexual encounters in her youth. She experimented more freely with her sexuality when she was a student, but as she was already in the process of reinventing herself at that time, her past self from this period does not correspond to her secret alter ego either. Natalie's most striking feature is that she attempts to live up to certain expectations that her society and family have, performing extremely well in different scenarios, but does not see to her own emotional needs. Essentially, Natalie plays different roles, but has no clear sense of who she actually is underneath it all.

FELIX COOPER

Felix is black working-class man who also lives in northwest London. He has previously struggled with problems such drug addiction and a difficult relationship with his unreliable mother. His father, Lloyd, on the other hand, has cared for him and his siblings with love. Another, more recent, positive person in his life is his girlfriend, Grace. Felix is now clean and attempts to move forward with his life. Grace encourages him forward, using methods such as telling him to write "a list of things he wanted from the universe" (p. 100). While Felix has his reservations about what this list could actually achieve, he is grateful to have a woman like Grace in his life. Felix goes to see an old lover from his past to tell her that he has found love and wants to build a life with his girlfriend, and will not come to see her again. Despite all his good intentions, Felix ends up having sex with the woman, but leaves her place determined not to go back. He feels happy with the way his life is going and is looking forward to his future, but he is robbed of this future as he is mugged and killed before he reaches home that day.

NATHAN BOGLE

Nathan Bogle is an old classmate of Leah's and Natalie's. He now lives on the street, is involved with crime and suffers from drug addiction. It is suggested that Nathan is responsible for Felix's death, or at least involved with the crime. In school he seemed very different from now. Leah was in love with him when she was a child, and he was generally liked. However, from an early age he has been aware that his future might not be very bright. His mother had told him that "Everyone loves a bredrin when he's ten. After that he's a problem. Can't stay ten always" (p. 313). While Natalie thinks that this is a horrible thing to say to a child, Nathan regards it as the simple truth. It is unclear how much these lines have been a self-fulfilling prophecy and how much they have been merely an uncomfortable truth, but they certainly describe Nathan's life experiences.

MICHEL

Michel is Leah's husband. He is French with African origins. He is a kind, handsome man who wishes to build a life with Leah and move up socially. He and Leah love each other, but they do not always understand one another or share the same values. Interestingly, this brings him closer to Leah's mother, with whom he initially did not have much in common: "Between Pauline and Michel there exists nothing but mistrust and misunderstanding except in this blessed alignment, once rare, now more frequent, in which Leah has been an idiot and this fact forms a coalition between natural enemies" (p. 18). Michel desperately wants children, and feels very betrayed when he finds out that Leah has been taking contraceptive pills behind his back.

FRANK DE ANGELIS

Frank is Natalie's husband. He is of Caribbean and Italian origin. His family is rather well off and his privileged background is very different from that of his wife. He is kind, successful and charming. Nevertheless, Natalie is not truly happy with him. It seems that despite their mutual attraction, they are unable to properly connect with each other on a deeper, emotional level.

SHAR

Shar is working-class woman living in northwest London. She is a drug addict, and scams Leah for money by claiming that her mother has had a heart attack. Although Leah is angry that she was lied to, she wishes to help Shar, as although she lied, her suffering is real. Shar refuses Leah's help. She represents a poor person who suffers from multiple problems, none of which are likely to be resolved.

PAULINE

Pauline is Leah's mother. She is an older Irish lady with a strong character. She and Leah represent very different generations with very different aspirations. Pauline is happy to see her daughter married, but would wish for grandchildren, which Leah does not provide her with (although Leah does not tell her mother that she does not want children).

MARCIA BLAKE

Marcia is Natalie's mother. She is a working-class Caribbean woman with strict religious values. Natalie and her mother do not seem to share a very close bond or to understand one another.

ANALYSIS

A PORTRAIT OF NORTHWEST LONDON

The novel's title, *NW*, refers to the postcode of northwest London. Most of the novel takes place in this area, which is the centre of its characters' world. The novel amounts to a collection of portraits of contemporary urban life in this area. Streets, buildings, the way people use language and their interests and life goals are brought to life in this stylistically experimental work of fiction. People living in the area described in *NW* are working-class people of different origins. As a novel describing people from this environment and social class, the novel is essentially about class. However, this is only one of the themes explored in the book. Zapata argues that "While it is certain that the concept of class is central in the novel, race, gender, and sexuality also disclose the interconnection of oppressing discourses present in the formation of subjects currently living under the influence of neocolonial and neoimperialist discourses"

(Zapata, 2014: 87). These themes are investigated in the context of a specific geographical and social space, but also have more universal connotations. The difficulty of social mobility is not only a problem faced by Londoners in the northwest part of the city, but this specific context adds a layer of meaning to the conversation.

SOCIAL CLASS

Social class is the novel's most obvious theme. The working-class people in it seem unable to break free from their social status or poverty. Characters such as Shar and Nathan Bogle, who struggle with poverty and addiction as well as being involved with crime, exemplify this tendency most clearly, but even Natalie Blake, who climbs up the social ladder very successfully, seems to be defined by her background, as she does not seem to feel quite at home in her new, privileged existence. Marcus argues that this novel, which uses many experimental narrative techniques, is rather pessimistic about social mobility: "This is not a freewheeling stream of consciousness about the mobilites of self invention but the painful immobilities of class"

(Marcus, 2013: 70). At the beginning of the novel, Leah hears an inspiring sentence: "On the radio: I am the sole author of the dictionary that defines me. A good line – write it out on the back of a magazine" (p. 3). This, however, seems to be only that: a good line, with little connection with reality. Marcus maintains that "We are not the sole authors of the dictionaries that define us; in fact, we are not, even in part, the authors of who we are" (Marcus, 2013: 70). By this he means that austerity, debt and other very real problems stand in the way of many people's aspirations. The theme of social class is investigated in connection with other social markers that define who one is. What it means to working-class is combined with other ways in which people are classified, such as what it means to be a man, a woman, English or an immigrant.

GENDER

Another important preoccupation of the novel is gender. Leah and Natalie face a certain set of expectations, and Felix another. Among the gender issues analysed in the novel are the expectation to have children, sexuality, and female identity. Leah does not fit into the mould of what is expected of her as a woman, as she does not want children and is attracted to other women. Although Leah is happily married to a man, her past female partner is still important to her, as she still thinks of her: "She once was a true love of mine. Now that girl is married, too" (p. 42). Leah and the girl have moved on, but the memory is still a vital part of who she is. It is significant that Leah keeps both her past female lovers and her not wanting to have children a secret from her husband, thus showing that it is not what is considered the norm. Zapata observes that "Leah does not fit into what is "normal" or, rather, heteronormative" (Zapata, 2014: 90). Society's expectations for a woman can thus still be rather traditional, even in our modern society.

Natalie too struggles with her sexuality, even if not in the same way as Leah. Natalie (or Keisha, as she was still called at the time) struggles with her sexual desires as a religious young woman. Zapata explains that "As a teenager, she considers herself to be a forgery after realising that she is full of inconsistencies and contradictory attitudes, such as her recently awakened sexuality and its repression by religious morality" (*ibid.*: 91). Although Natalie rejects her religious upbringing as an adult, her issues with sexuality seem to remain unresolved, as she continues to explore her sexuality in extramarital relationships. Neither Leah or Natalie feel what they 'are supposed to feel' as women, and this leads to them feeling outside of society's norms.

MULTICULTURALITY AND RACE

Another remarkable feature of *NW* is its richness of characters of different races and ethnicities. The experience of being black in a predominately white society is explored, for example, through Natalie's experiences when studying law. Leah, on the other hand, is the only white person at her work. The consequences of colonisation, immigration and other issues connected with race and ethnicity are dealt with in relation with other social issues such as class. Leah and Michel, the interracial couple, are of different races, but joined in their social status: "Nothing in Leah's childhood prepared her for the frequency with which she now attends dinner parties, most often at Natalie's house, where she and Michel are

invited to provide something like local colour"
(p. 85). Zapata maintains that "they seem to have
been colonized by those belonging now to the
upper classes, who speak for them, dissect their
lives and limit their agency" (Zapata, 2014: 88).
Smith herself has said that "colonialism is all
about class" (quoted in Zapata, 2014: 88). This,
of course, does not mean that race is irrelevant,
but that it should be analysed in connection with
other factors.

IDENTITY

NW also investigates identity. The factors described above – class, race and gender – can be
building blocks of one's identity, but ultimately
it is something more complex, as can be obser-
ved from Natalie's experiences: "Daughter drag.
Sister drag. Mother drag. Wife drag. Court drag.
Rich drag. Poor drag. British drag. Jamaican drag.
Each required a different wardrobe. But when
considering these various attitudes she struggled to think what would be the most authen-
tic, or perhaps the least inauthentic" (p. 278).
Zapata argues that "The metaphor of "drag"
is used here not only for gender, but also for

Natalie's disguises in terms of class, nationality and the private/public divide, exposing them as constructions" (Zapata, 2014: 92). Natalie seems to be performing all aspects of her identity to such an extent that she seems to lack a stable identity altogether.

ADULTHOOD AND THE PASSAGE OF TIME

Another of the novel's themes is adulthood and the passage of time. Leah seems to be particularly affected by these issues: "She fears the destination. Be objective! What is the fear? It is something to do with death and time and age. Simply: I am eighteen in my mind I am eighteen and if I do nothing if I stand still nothing will change I will be eighteen always. For always. Time will stop. I'll never die" (p. 24). Her unwillingness to move forward and have children is connected with this dilemma. Leah fears death, aging and being an adult, which might be seen as common problem within people of her generation. Smith's handling of the issue highlights not just a generational issue, but also a very human feeling of fear of death.

STYLE

The novel's style is one of its most remarkable aspects. *NW* is highly experimental. It mixes relatively straightforward third-person realistic narration with metafictional devices (fiction conscious of itself and its fictionality) and techniques typical of literary modernism. Modernism in arts (including literature) can be understood as the movement of renewal and experimentation that took place in the late 19th and the early 20th century (it reached its prime after the First World War). Modernist literature sought to depart from classical or traditional forms, is characterised by the use of experimental literary devices, and emphasises individual, subjective experiences. The most obvious modernistic technique that Smith uses in this novel is stream of consciousness, which can be understood as a literary style which attempts to depict the flow of thoughts as they occur instead of organising them in a logical or linear fashion. For example, observe the flow of thought in the following passage: "Pencil leaves no mark on magazine pages. Somewhere she has read that the gloss gives you cancer. Everyone knows it shouldn't be this hot.

Shrivelled blossom and bitter little apples. Birds singing the wrong tunes in the wrong trees too early in the year. Don't you bloody start! Look up: the girl's burnt paunch rests on the railing" (p. 3).

Regarding the mix of styles, Guignery observes that "Chapters 9 and 10 are a brilliant juxtaposition of contemporary technology and modernist narration: while the former is a pastiche of Google Map-type factual direction instructions to walk from point A to point B, the latter is its stream-of-consciousness alter ego" (Guignery, 2013). She further comments on the novel's style by stating that Smith "combines modernist strategies with a typically postmodernist tendency to draw attention to the mechanisms of novel-writing, without letting go completely of the road of realism" *(ibid.)*. This observation sums up the most elements of the novel's stylistic mix. This mix supports the novel's content: the multitude of styles mirrors London's layers of cultures, places and different kinds of people.

FURTHER REFLECTION

- Discuss the depiction of London in the novel. How is the city, or parts of it, experienced by the different characters?
- Discuss the role of social class in the novel.
- Discuss the different ways in which the novel's characters are marginalised. What role do features such as class, race, ethnicity, religion, gender and sexuality play in this?
- Discuss the difficulties Leah (and other characters) has in adapting to adulthood and accepting aging. Is this typical for her generation? Why (not)?
- In your opinion, why is Natalie/Keisha not satisfied with the life she has worked so hard to build?
- In your opinion, what is the function of Felix's story? Does it make victims of violent crime in neighbourhoods such as his more human and more visible?

- Discuss the representation of female sexuality in the novel.
- Discuss the novel's experimental style. What do you think Smith wishes to achieve with the stylistic devices she uses?

We want to hear from you!
Leave a comment on your online library
and share your favourite books on social media!

FURTHER READING

REFERENCE EDITION

- Smith, Z. (2013) *NW*. London: Penguin Books.

REFERENCE STUDIES

- Guignery, V. (2013) Zadie Smith's *NW*: the Novel at an 'anxiety crossroads'?. *Études britanniques contemporaines*. [Online]. [Accessed 31 March 2019]. Available from: <https://journals.openedi-tion.org/ebc/996>
- Marcus, D. (2013) Post-Hysterics: Zadie Smith and the Fiction of Austerity. *Dissent*. 60(2), pp. 67-73.
- Zapata, B. P. (2014) 'In Drag': Performativity and Authenticity in Zadie Smith's NW. *International Studies: Interdisciplinary Political and Cultural Journal*. 16(1), pp. 83-95.
- (2019) Zadie Smith. *British Council*. [Online]. [Accessed 31 March 2019]. Available from: <https://literature.britishcouncil.org/writer/zadie-smith>

ADAPTATIONS

- *NW*. (2016) [Film]. Saul Dibb. Dir. UK: BBC.

www.brightsummaries.com

Ebook EAN: 9782808019835

Paperback EAN: 9782808019842

Legal Deposit: D/2019/12603/156

Cover: © Primento

Digital conception by Primento, the digital partner of publishers.